Holy Island

A Visitor's Guide

**Funding raised by
The National Lottery**
and awarded by the Heritage Lottery Fund

heritage
lottery fund
LOTTERY FUNDED

PEREGRINI Lindisfarne
Landscape Partnership

Northumberland Coast AONB Partnership
www.northumberlandcoastaonb.org

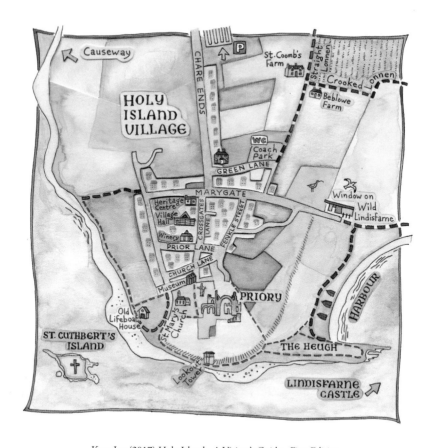

Kerr, Ian (2017) Holy Island - A Visitor's Guide - First Edition
Northumberland Coast AONB Partnership, Morpeth.
ISBN 978 1 87340 239 8
A catalogue record of this book is available from the British Library.
This book was written and compiled by Ian Kerr on behalf of the
Peregrini Lindisfarne Landscape Partnership.

Published by Northumberland Coast AONB Partnership,
County Hall, Morpeth, Northumberland, NE61 2EF

Cover Photo by Emma Rothera
www.emmarotheraphotography.com

Maps by Sarah Farooqi
www.sarahfarooqi.co.uk

Designed and produced by Printspot
www.print-spot.co.uk

Contents

Introduction

With its rich religious history and stunning landscapes, Holy Island is one of the jewels of the Northumberland Coast Area of Outstanding Natural Beauty (AONB). It is also one of the most popular, attracting up to 700,000 visitors annually.

They can enjoy an island of wide horizons under big skies, a place with its own special qualities of tranquillity and spirituality, particularly when cut off twice daily by the tide. The picturesque village, cradle of Christianity in the north, has a wide range of places of interest. This guide aims to help with information about them. When visiting is over or a break is needed, the local cafes, pubs and hotels ensure a very warm welcome.

In contrast, the rest of the island is a place of peace, much of it part of the Lindisfarne National Nature Reserve. It has superb beaches, sand dunes and dramatic rocky headlands giving spectacular views. There are lonely salt marshes and huge areas of inter-tidal sand and mud teeming with wildlife. These are places to really get away from it all.

The special qualities of the coastline between the port of Amble and the historic Border town of Berwick upon Tweed led to its designation as an Area of Outstanding Natural Beauty in 1958. Such status is awarded only to areas of England and Wales considered to have the finest landscapes. The designation aims to promote the conservation and enhancement of their special characters.

The AONB has 21 Scheduled Monuments, including the castles on Holy Island and at Bamburgh, Dunstanburgh and Warkworth. It also has 229 Listed Buildings, two Registered Parks and Gardens and eight Conservation Areas, including the island. It carries out a wide range of duties, including the provision of the Northumberland Coast Path which covers 62 miles of beautiful land and seascapes between Cresswell in the south and Berwick.

Peregrini Lindisfarne Landscape Partnership, funded by the Heritage Lottery Fund, is a partnership of community, voluntary and public organisations. It aims to provide a wide range of conservation and public engagement projects on the island and adjacent mainland. This involves local people working to protect, restore and enhance landscapes and assist with economic regeneration.

Please enjoy your visit and return again soon!

Ian Kerr
Author

History

From hunter-gatherers to saints and sinner and early tourists

Although Holy Island is famed for its saints, the Lindisfarne Gospels and Viking raids, its history goes back to the wake of the last Ice Age more than 10,000 years ago. Britain was still joined to Europe, today's island was part of the mainland and the sea was three or four miles further east.

Tantalising evidence of human presence in a very different world comes from 2,000 pieces of worked flint recovered around the old limestone quarry at Nessend. They include tiny fragments of arrow-heads from the earliest days of Mesolithic hunter-gatherers around 8,500BC to leaf-shaped arrow-heads from the Neolithic, showing local activity spanning 6,000 years.

When rising seas cut off Britain around 6,000 years ago the island, as it then became, was still inhabited. Discoveries include a Bronze Age spearhead and pottery fragments from the Roman period when the island was known as Medcaut, a Celtic name of unknown origin.

The next evidence comes from the island's religious history when the Kingdom of Northumbria was ruled by Oswald from his capital at Bamburgh. As a child, Oswald became a Christian while exiled in south west Scotland where he met Irish monks from

St. Aidan Statue © Ian Cooke

Iona. Deciding that his pagan subjects could benefit from conversion, he invited Aidan and 15 monks to settle on the island in 635AD. Aidan was the first inhabitant whose name we know. By that stage it was known as Lindisfarne. The name may have come from a small river, the Lindis, which flowed into the flats with "farne," meaning island, being added.

Everything known about Aidan comes from that wonderful early medieval chronicler, Bede. Aidan established a monastery on the Irish pattern, probably a wooden church, dwelling huts and a larger communal building, perhaps on the site now occupied by Lindisfarne Priory and the parish church although excavations in 2017 indicate that an early church was established on the Heugh. Converting the local inhabitants would have been a challengingly dangerous mission, particularly as he couldn't speak the language. Oswald helped as an interpreter and perhaps the royal presence ensured large and respectful audiences.

Volunteers excavating foundations on the Heugh © *Jessica Turner*

Aidan died at Bamburgh around 651 and is credited with firmly establishing Christianity in the north. He was eclipsed by one of his successors, Cuthbert, whose name is synonymous with Lindisfarne. Born near Melrose, he was first a shepherd and then a soldier and entered Melrose Abbey becoming prior in 662. It was a time of great upheaval between Roman and Celtic churches. When the Synod of Whitby in 664 decided in favour of the Roman tradition he was sent to Lindisfarne to ease the transition.

Around 676 he took up the simpler life of a hermit. Tradition says he spent time on the rocky tidal outcrop, St Cuthbert's Island, just a stones throw from the monastery. He certainly spent considerable periods on Inner Farne. There it's claimed he laid down rules to protect nesting Eider ducks, making him Britain's first conservationist by a millennium or so. Eiders are still referred to locally as St Cuthbert's or Cuddy's ducks. The old Northumbrian name for a horse, a "Cuddy", may also be connected with him.

Cuthbert died on Inner Farne in 687. Two flaming torches were waved by attendants as the pre-arranged signal of his death and were seen by monks watching from a tower on the Heugh. Recent excavations have shown the foundations of several buildings, perhaps one of them the tower.

His body was returned to Lindisfarne for burial. Astonishingly, 11 years later it was found to be incorrupt, more like a sleeping man than a corpse. A miracle was claimed, he was declared a saint and his grave became a magnet for pilgrims. The Cult of Cuthbert was born. The Lindisfarne Gospels by one of his successors, Eadfrith, were produced in tribute.

793 is regarded as the start of the Viking era and Lindisfarne became their first target in England. The best-known account in the Anglo-Saxon Chronicle recalls:

"In that year terrible portents appeared over Northumbria and miserably frightened the inhabitants: these were exceptional flashes of lightning and fiery dragons were seen flying in the air. A great famine soon followed and a little after that in the same year on 8 June the harrying of the heathen miserably destroyed God's church on Lindisfarne by rapine and slaughter."

If fiery dragons and apocalyptic warning are hard to swallow, a more prosaic account was provided by a 12th Century monk, Symeon of Durham:

"They came to the church of Lindisfarne, laid everything waste with grievous plunder, trampled the holy places with polluted feet, dug up the altars and seized all the treasures of the holy church. They killed some of the brothers: some they took away in fetters: many they drove out naked and loaded with insults, some they drowned in the sea."

That first raid sent shock waves through Christendom. Others followed and in 875 the monks decided that island life was untenable. They left taking Cuthbert's body, the Gospels and Aidan's bones. Island historian Canon Kate Tristram says the community was powerful and wealthy. We should forget romantic notions of a few panicking, tattered monks wandering the countryside with Cuthbert's body. In reality, it was a carefully planned retreat and relocation. They went first to the Tweed Valley, then to Cumbria and Yorkshire.

The community then settled for more than a century at Chester-le-Street and finally moved in 1104 to the newly built Durham Cathedral where Cuthbert's body has remained.

At Durham, Cuthbert's body remained intact and no doubt his arrival was welcomed. A miracle-working saint was very good for business in attracting pilgrims and their cash. Cuthbert's influence has continued ever since. A simple check of local telephone directories shows twice as many organisations bearing Cuthbert's name compared with Aidan. It seems that Aidan's biggest mistake was to turn into a skeleton while Cuthbert remained intact.

Benedictine monks occupied the island by 1120 to create an offshoot of Durham. Under the patronage of England's new rulers, the Normans, the Priory was built. Shortly afterwards, the beautiful church of St Mary the Virgin was built alongside and remains to this day a destination of pilgrims. The island acquired its modern name with monks referring to it as Insula Sancta, a reference to its religious reputation.

Everything changed again in 1536 with Henry VIII's dissolution of the monasteries. The Priory was used as a military store during conflicts between England and Scotland and some of its stone was taken to build Lindisfarne Castle.

The island's military significance was demonstrated in 1543 when as part of plans to invade Scotland, 2,500 soldiers landed and ten warships anchored in the harbour, then much larger. The old shoreline is still visible by going through the revolving gates near the Crown & Anchor pub and crossing Sanctuary Close. The steep bank on the left marks the old shoreline. By 1559 the Castle was manned by a garrison of more than 20 soldiers.

The first known island map was made in 1611 by John Speed, a protégé of Queen Elizabeth I. It showed features familiar today. The Priory was depicted as the "Abbey," the village was rather grandly described as the "Towne" and the Market Place with its medieval cross was depicted. Across the island was the instantly recognisable "freshwater Loughe" and the "Snewke or Coney Warren", a reference to its use for rearing rabbits. Sandham Bay was Sandon Bay, a name still widely used today, and it was flooded by the "German Ocean", a name which dropped out of fashion with the First World War.

In the 19th Century the herring industry provided a brief economic boom for the island, as did quarrying and lime-making. However, the islanders were generally left to get on with their normal activities of fishing and farming.

Eight local men died during the Great War and three more in the Second World War. Reminders of the latter are lines of anti-invasion blocks at Beal shore and concrete pillboxes at Beal Point. The wide beaches at Goswick were used as a practice range and the tides still occasionally reveal unexploded bombs.

Other effects of the war were brought home to islanders twice during 1941. In May, a Junkers bomber, damaged during a raid on Glasgow, made a forced landing on the North Shore. The crew set fire to it before the island's Home Guard rounded them up. But enough was left for every island child to grab souvenirs.

Then on a cold November morning islanders were surprised to find five wet, hungry and exhausted young men scrambling ashore from an open boat on rocks along the Castle road. After it was confirmed they weren't Germans, they told an incredible story. Five days earlier they had stolen the boat and fuel. Under cover of darkness, they'd slipped out of the Norwegian port of Kristiansand, evading German shore batteries and naval patrols. They had made their way across the North Sea avoiding minefields and other hazards until the Castle loomed from the darkness. By that stage they hardly cared where they were because they were so tired and seasick.

They were taken to the Lindisfarne Hotel and given a meal, dry clothes and cigarettes while the Norwegian Free Forces in Britain were alerted. That night a coded radio message informed the Norwegian resistance of their success. The wartime annals of Norway are filled with similar attempted escapes. Many small boats vanished, the North Sea proving as deadly an enemy as the Germans. Sadly, four of the five died in action. A memorial seat presented in 2010 by their families is near the spot they gratefully came ashore.

Sudden changes have always marked the island's history. The opening of the Causeway in 1954, followed soon afterwards by piped water and electricity, were all huge changes. A few days after the Causeway opened people rushed from their homes as word spread that a motor coach was approaching the village. The modern era had arrived. Nothing would ever be the same again.

Arriving at Holy Island. 11257.

The Village Today

Many first-time visitors, particularly those from outside the area, are surprised at the size of the island, having merely seen photographs of its iconic Castle and arrive expecting a northern version of St Michael's Mount. Others visualise a quiet picture postcard village and a few fishing boats.

The reality is very different. They find instead a busy vibrant community. The village has two hotels, two pubs, a new village hall, a village store, heritage centre, two museums, a winery, art gallery and a scriptorium. There are cafes, coffee shops and gift shops and Anglican, Roman Catholic and United Reform churches. There's a twice weekly bus service to and from Berwick which increases to operate daily during the summer school holiday period. A shuttle bus links the car parks, village and Castle.

There are numerous bed and breakfast establishments and many holiday cottages and houses. Parties of youngsters are catered for at a camp run

The Village Today © Gavin Duthie

by the St Vincent de Paul Society (SVP). National organisations include English Heritage, responsible for the Priory and the National Trust which has the Castle and a shop.

At a time when many small villages have lost most of their services, Holy Island with a resident population of around 200, has prospered. Most of its services are heavily dependent on tourism although there are still reminders of an earlier life. Hunter-gatherers were the first inhabitants and they are still represented by the last of their kind, fishermen. Five fast modern boats provide full-time livelihoods for a dozen men. They specialise in crabs and lobsters, many exported to Europe. The island's two working farms provide further employment.

Like other rural communities, today's greater mobility and the need to move away for jobs, means there are far fewer native islanders. But family roots remain strong, as does the lure of home. When one family organised a reunion via the internet they attracted visitors from America, Canada, Australia and Germany. All could trace their ancestry to an island sea captain of the early 1700s. Every two or three years there's a reunion for women who were in the island school six decades ago, one travelling from Canada to attend.

Tourism is nothing new, only the scale has changed. The earliest visitors were sportsmen coming to shoot on the flats. During the 18th Century that involved travelling by coach to Belford and then walking to the flats. In the 19th and first half of the 20th Centuries, trains were met at Beal station by horse-drawn traps to carry visitors across the sands. Later, old taxis with high chassis were bought by enterprising islanders to provide a regular service.

As long ago as 1908 the then island schoolmaster produced visitor guides and postcards of island girls and fishermen, dressed in their Sunday best for the camera. Wealthy families would take houses for the summer.

There was no running water or power but, surprisingly, there was a golf course in the dunes at Chare Ends. It wasn't just any old golf course but one designed by an early sporting legend, a five-times winner of the Open Championship, James Braid, who also planned the famed courses at Gleneagles and Carnoustie. It opened in 1907, thanks to support from wealthy locals who wanted their guests to enjoy a game. The course fell into disuse in the 1950s and was quickly reclaimed by nature.

The gentle tempo changed with the opening of the Causeway. That first coach which so excited the villager set the trend for mass tourism. Some visitors are attracted by the island's historic and religious connections, others by its wildlife. Most come simply because it's a wonderful place or because they've seen it on television or in films. Many regular visitors recall visits to the SVP camp as their first and lasting experience. At one time the island was a summer attraction but now it's a year-round destination.

One organisation has worked tirelessly to improve the village. The Holy Island of Lindisfarne Community Development Trust is made up of representatives of county and parish councils, the Fishermen's Society, village hall, churches, school and local businesses. Working in close co-operation with other groups it has attracted funding for a wide range of projects.

Achievements include affordable housing for 11 island families. With Natural England it helped provide the Lookout and Window on Wild Lindisfarne projects while with Peregrini Lindisfarne improvements to the harbour and the opening of Lifeboat Museum were achieved. It and its partners are engaged in continuous programmes of improvements.

Window on Wild Lindisfarne

Around the Village

History all around

The village has three sites of great religious significance: The Priory, the Parish Church of St Mary the Virgin and St Cuthbert's Island. The priory and the church have always been thought to be on the site of Aidan's first church. The island's most famous surviving religious artefact, the Lindisfarne Gospels, is celebrated with an exhibition at the local heritage centre. All are very close together, making them easy to take in with a gentle stroll.

Aerial view of village, Priory and Heugh excavations © Richard Carlton

Lindisfarne Priory

The most spectacular religious ruin in Northumberland lies in the shelter of the Heugh. Its red sandstone walls, pillars and iconic rainbow arch have been mellowed and weathered by ten centuries of wind and rain.

The Priory was established by the Benedictines who arrived around 1120. There are striking similarities with the architecture of Durham Cathedral. That's no coincidence as its bishops ordered its construction when England was settling down under its new masters, the Normans. They

The Priory © Robert Turner

regarded themselves as the true inheritors of the traditions of Aidan and Cuthbert. Teams of masons who completed the magnificent cathedral may have moved north to work on the Priory.

The Priory, now managed by English Heritage, must have been a very busy place in its heyday. The ruins contain evidence of a thriving domestic scene with a bakery, brew house and guest accommodation as well as areas for worship. Villagers and laymen would not have been allowed to worship there so the parish church was built alongside.

It's not known how many people were in occupation, perhaps a prior and a dozen or so monks. But with pilgrims and guests there would be a constant demand for food which probably resulted in the development of the village. Fish, shellfish, geese, ducks and other birds figure prominently on the Priory tables.

The monks may have introduced rabbits to supply a year-round source of meat and skins and may also have begun oyster farming. Legend has it that they paid a hundred shillings for a boatload of oysters to launch the business. Oyster farming was reintroduced to the flats in 1989. Now Lindisfarne oysters feature on island menus as well as those of some top provincial and London restaurants.

The monks were probably the first people to dig for coal and produce lime, both activities which continued sporadically until the 19th Century. A modern sculpture of St Cuthbert by Fenwick Lawson stands in the grounds. Because of his supposed connections with Eider ducks, one peeps out from the hem of his robe.

Religious occupation ended suddenly with Henry VIII's Dissolution of the Monasteries and the Priory gradually fell into disrepair. What remains today is the result of restoration in the 19th and 20th Centuries.

The Priory museum contains an impressive collection, including Anglo-Saxon stonework, crosses, grave markers and a famous piece of carving known as the "Viking Raiders" or the "Warrior Stone". It shows a procession of warriors, weapons aloft. Various theories have emerged of what it actually represents, ranging from the Vikings to an image of Doomsday as described in the Scriptures.

St Mary's Church

Aidan's wooden settlement was followed by a stone church during the Anglo-Saxon period. In turn, this was replaced when the Benedictines created the Priory. Like most ancient churches, it has changed radically to reach its present beautiful form but there are still traces of Anglo-Saxon stonework. The wall above the chancel arch shows the line of an earlier narrower arch.

St. Mary's Church © Emma Rothera

The bell tower which gives the church today's distinctive shape was added in 1723 but after that period it went through ruinous times. Part of the chancel roof collapsed and a 19th Century visitor complained that although the island had nine public houses, the church was in a sorry state. It was cold, damp and musty, the walls covered in green mould and the floor running with insects. Shortly afterwards, things improved. With typical Victorian zeal, the roof was restored, walls were repaired and plastered and a new porch was built which still serves as the main entrance. An older porch which provided a mortuary for bodies from the sea was closed off. Stained glass windows were fitted and the church emerged in its present form.

Today's visitor entering the church and glancing right can receive a shock to their senses: a larger than life black wooden artwork - "The Journey" where sculptor Fenwick Lawson depicts six monks carrying a replica of Cuthbert's open coffin. It's a striking introduction to the building. On the chancel wall is a small inscribed plaque, a poignant reminder of the Viking raid of 739. It's a humble apology from Norway presented in 1993, the 1,200th anniversary of the event. It depicts St Olav who helped bring Christianity to Norway and contributed to the end of the Viking era.

Old traditions are still observed, particular with island weddings, always huge celebrations. In the churchyard, near the striking sculpture of St Aidan, is the Petting Stone, the large base of a medieval cross. By tradition, a new island bride, helped by two fishermen, jumps over the stone as a local fertility rite. A villager who found an elderly lady resting on the stone left her in giggling bemusement when he pointed out the possible consequences. Wedding celebrations don't end there. As the new couple pass through the church gate they pass between lines of islanders with shotguns who fire fusillades over their heads.

The broad lane leading to the church's western gate is Fiddlers' Green which these days has fine houses looking across a wide grassed area. They're a far cry from the humble fishing cottages they replaced. The name Fiddlers' Green has close associations with the sea. Immortalised in folk song, it's the place fishermen hope to go after death, a maritime paradise.

THE OTHER CHURCHES

The island has a United Reform church, now the St Cuthbert's Centre, just off Fiddlers' Green and its Roman Catholic church, St Aidan's, opposite the Post Office in Green Lane.

St Cuthbert's opened in 1892 to cater for Presbyterian islanders. In 1972 it became part of the United Reform Church. In 2000 it became the St Cuthbert's Centre, providing not just a place of worship but a quiet retreat for pilgrims and visitors and an exhibition space for both religious and secular functions. A minister is based on the island.

The modern Roman Catholic presence on the island was established at Lindisfarne House where one room was used as a chapel. The need for a church became pressing after the opening of the Causeway, a huge increase in visitors and the opening of the adjoining St Vincent de Paul camp. An appeal for funds was launched and the present building was opened on Easter Day 2007. A priest from Seahouses carries out services and there is a resident pastoral assistant.

St Cuthbert's Island

One of the most fascinating corners of the village is this tiny tidal island, links with an earlier way of life and the Lifeboat Museum. As far as youngsters are concerned, there's something much more exciting - treasure. The small island, as its name implies, has close links with St Cuthbert.

St. Cuthbert's Island © Gavin Duthie

Although his quest for solitude took him periodically to Inner Farne, it could be achieved here much more conveniently. Anyone in retreat could be supplied with food and drink, an important consideration unless fasting was involved.

The island is accessible at low tide although great care is needed as the rocks are slippery. A modern wooden cross marks the site of a small square cell, now nothing more than a grassy humped outline. Cuthbert was believed to occupy this cell although it's debatable whether the existing sparse remains date back to his period or are later. Whatever the truth, the high top of the island gives fine views across the flats with the prospect of very close glimpses of passing seals.

Just through the gate is Jenny Bell's Well, one of the handful of places villagers had to draw water before the piped supply was provided. It was a daily household chore, still remembered by older islanders. Children would often get the job as well as visiting the farm for milk and eggs. The stone surround has been excavated and restored.

The small beach in front is a favourite spot for searching for St Cuthbert's Beads. They are the tiny, flat fossilised portions of the stems of crinoids of the Carboniferous period 300 million years ago. With a central hole, they can be threaded to form a necklace. Tradition has it that Cuthbert used them as a rosary although the first mention of that doesn't appear to have emerged until the 17th Century. It may be yet another legend surrounding the island's most famous saint.

In other parts of Britain these beads are known as "fairy money" while in Germany they are named after another saint, Boniface. Digging in the sand for them is an occupation which can keep youngsters entertained for hours.

The Gospels and their peaceful garden

The Lindisfarne Centre with its Gospels exhibition and the Gospel Garden are just 50 yards apart in Marygate, the village's broad main street.

The exhibition includes a facsimile, opened to show two pages of the exquisite early medieval artwork of this national treasure. There is also an interactive version where visitors can turn the pages and hear spoken extracts. They can enlarge the text to examine the original Latin and the Anglo-Saxon script added later between the lines.

The Gospel Garden © Gavin Duthie

The Gospels were produced in homage to St Cuthbert by one of his successors, Eadfrith. The Gospels are on calfskin and 130 young animals would have been needed to provide the 258 pages. Experts have also calculated that a modern calligrapher, working in a warm, well-lit studio with modern inks and equipment, would have to work full-time for two years to replicate the work. Eadfrith probably had to work by daylight or with candles and tallow lamps in far from comfortable conditions. He would have to have sourced the skins and his pens and brushes and produced his own inks from plant dyes and ground up rock. At one time it was thought that some of the vivid blues came from lapis lazuli, a bright semi-precious stone which would have indicated unlikely links with Asia.

Recent research shows that the colours came from a more humble source, woad, the plant which provided the blue body paint of the Celts which so fascinated the Romans.

The Gospels were obviously well hidden from the Vikings and were taken by the monks when they left the island. They were kept for centuries at Cuthbert's Shrine at Durham but ended up in private ownership after the Dissolution of the Monasteries. They were eventually placed in the British Library where they remain. Various suggestions that they should "come home" to Durham or even the island have fallen on deaf ears. But they have been on show in both Newcastle and Durham, each time attracting thousands. The Centre also has displays of island heritage and the Vikings.

The Gospel Garden provides a quiet oasis of peace from the bustle of the village. Inspired by the vivid colours of the manuscript, the garden was Newcastle City Council's entry for the 2003 Chelsea Flower Show where it won a silver medal. Normally such an exhibit would be dismantled and forgotten. In this case it was painstakingly moved to the island and reconstructed on the site of a disused allotment. Another sculpture by Fenwick Lawson, The Wheel Cross, showing the face of Cuthbert, is part of the display.

The Gospel Garden © Gavin Duthie

Lifeboats
A story of heroes and heroines

Few people are held in higher regard than lifeboatmen. Holy Island has a long and proud history, the last of its ten lifeboats, the Gertrude, having been withdrawn from service in 1967 ending almost two centuries of saving lives at sea.

Local lifeboat history dates back to 1786 when private organisations began to provide boats. From the time the Royal National Lifeboat Institution (RNLI) took over in 1865 and accurate records were kept, island boats carried out 205 missions and saved 336 lives. The island's most famous boat, the Lizzie Porter, now has pride of place at the Historic Dockyard at Chatham where she's the centre of its lifeboat display.

The last surviving station is now the island's Lifeboat Museum and contains displays and fascinating memorabilia. Among local documents is one which gives rare official recognition to the vital role played by island women in the dramatic rescue of nine men from the Hartlepool trawler, James B Graham, which smashed ashore on rocks near Emmanuel Head in January 1922.

Rescuers ran a mile across the island but couldn't get a line to her so needed the Lizzie Porter. There was a major problem: the tide was out and her carriage sank deep into the sand as efforts were made to drag her 50 yards into the sea. More than 30 women and girls rushed from their homes and with a massive effort got her afloat, some up to their necks in water.

Detail of the terracotta tile © Robert Turner

The RNLI gave a special award naming all the women. In rather flowery language it compared them with Grace Darling of Farne Islands fame, adding: "The action reflects infinite credit not merely on themselves, but on the women of our maritime race."

The women chose Daisy Cromarty, then 29, to go to London to accept the award. Islander Thelma Tough, who remembered Daisy when she was in her eighties, recalls: "She was physically strong and a natural leader. I can just imagine her yelling 'Howay girls, we can do it. When I say pull, then you pull.' That's the sort of person she was."

The last lifeboat station was under the Heugh. It was elevated with a greased ramp so the boat could slide into the sea at any stage of the tide. Greasing the ramp was often done by island boys who, inevitably, often ended up with much of the grease on themselves. The station was demolished after the Gertrude was withdrawn. It was felt, although islanders didn't agree, that lifeboats from Seahouses and Berwick could cover the area. The Gertrude was sold and is still in use as a pleasure craft in Cornwall.

Former Lifeboat House © Robert Turner

High Points of the Island

Two features dominate the south coast of the island, the Heugh and Beblowe Crag on which the Castle now proudly stands. Both consist of dolerite, very dark hard volcanic rock laid down 300 million years ago. It survived when softer rocks were ground away by successive ice ages, seas and weather.

These spectacular features are part of the Whin Sill which outcrops across Northumberland. Some of the most impressive stretches of the Roman Wall are built on its crests and it also provides the rock on which Bamburgh Castle was built. Offshore, it provides the Farne Islands.

THE HEUGH – Lookout on Wild Lindisfarne

The former Coastguard watchtower on the western end of the Heugh was built in the 1940s next to the remains of an 18th Century building, the Lantern Chapel. That name is misleading as it never had a religious function but was simply an earlier watch-point.

Coastguards used it in bad weather to look out for ships in trouble. Older islanders recall long spells of duty during storms. If there was a problem they would have to run down to the village and raise the alarm. When full-time coastguards needed a break, island boys were paid ten shillings (50p) to cover six-hour shifts. They considered it good pocket money. Radar, radio and other aids made the tower redundant.

Lookout on Wild Lindisfarne © Gavin Duthie

It has now been transformed as the Lookout on Wild Lindisfarne and provides panoramic views across the island, flats and far beyond. It includes imaginative displays about history and local wildlife. Line drawings on the window ledge provide information about what lies in front, depending on the tides.

Southwards is Guile Point with its twin brick 19th Century navigation pillars and a small building known as the Chapel. It too doesn't seem to have had religious use. South east are the Farne Islands and Bamburgh Castle. South west is Cheviot, Northumberland's highest hill, often snow-covered between October and April.

Looking south to Guile Point with the Cheviot Hills in the distance © Gavin Duthie

With binoculars the views are even more rewarding. To the north west is Berwick and the famous Royal Border railway bridge while northwards, on clear days, it's possible to see the white buildings of St Abbs Head, 25 miles away.

Just east of the tower is the island's simple war memorial, designed by Sir Edwin Lutyens, better known for transforming the Castle. After the Remembrance Day services in the parish church a procession winds its way across Sanctuary Close and up to the memorial. The names of the island's dead are read out, wreathes are laid and the one-minute silence is observed. It's a dramatic setting with only the sound of wind and waves, so different from the noise and chaos which robbed the island of some of its sons.

OSBORNE'S FORT – a precaution against pirates

Osborne's Fort © Robert Turner

At the eastern end of the Heugh, a broken-down tower and stretches of wall are all that remains of this little fort. Although the centuries-old conflicts with Scotland ended with the Act of Union, there was anxiety during the 17th Century about attacks from Dutch privateers. Defences were arranged accordingly.

The fort with walls three feet thick to withstand cannon fire was built in 1675. Old prints show how it looked. It was roughly triangular with a two-storey tower, the upper floor reached by an outside staircase. Its most important feature was a gun platform. It was designed to operate in co-operation with the gun battery at the Castle. Any hostile vessel venturing into the harbour, then much wider, would have been caught in withering crossfire. History doesn't record whether any privateers risked it. The fort became redundant during the 1700s and has since gradually collapsed, parts eroded by the sea.

Today only parts of the tower's lower sections are standing and work has been carried out to prevent further deterioration. On the southern flank, parts of the fort's thick walls remain and are dominated by wild flowers and grasses. The wall now serves a much more peaceful service as a sheltered backrest for benches which allow visitors quiet and sunny views towards Ross and Bamburgh. Other parts of the site are nothing more than grassy humps.

UPTURNED BOATS – a reminder of the herring trade

Just below the old fort is the island's pier and the Ouse, centre of today's fishing. The upturned boats which line the shore are another of the island's iconic features and are a reminder of the glory days of the 19th Century herring industry. At its height in the 1860s, massive shoals of the "Silver Darlings" of song and folklore were pursued by hundreds of boats as they migrated southwards. The industry didn't just provide employment for fishermen but for a travelling army of women and girls, skilled at gutting the herrings and packing them in barrels of brine. They followed the fleets from Scotland to Yorkshire. Salted fish were sent to markets across Britain and northern Europe, particularly the Baltic countries. Others were preserved by smoking, the smokehouses providing rough and ready accommodation for the "Herring Girls".

Upturned Boats © Gavin Duthie

At its peak around 36 island boats were involved but scores of others also used the harbour to unload their catches and to get back to sea as quickly as possible. It was all too good to last. Exploitation on such a massive scale was totally unsustainable and by the late 1870s it was in decline. It was virtually gone by the turn of the 20th Century.

One by one, the island's large boats were hauled ashore, the last in 1914. They were upturned, cut in half and fitted with doors to create the picturesque sheds of today. One old island photograph shows another being used to house a family although that seems to have been an isolated case. The sheds have been preserved with repeated coatings of tar, giving their black appearance although recently one has been transformed to bright blue. Some are still owned by fishing families, others by the owners of pleasure craft which now outnumber fishing vessels.

Another reminder is the Herring House, the large three-sided building behind the upturned boats. Now transformed into properties with stunning sea views, it started life much more humbly as a smokehouse. Others existed in the village and have also been converted into homes.

THE CASTLE – from gun battery to stately home

The Castle began life in the 16th Century with an urgent Royal decree: "All Havens should be fenced with bulwarks and blockhouses against the Scots". Holy Island was an important Tudor harbour and its defence against Scotland, then flexing its military muscle, was essential.

The initial development was of two cannon platforms, probably constructed with stone from the Priory. The battery was manned by two master gunners, one master's mate and around 20 soldiers. It was a garrison maintained for many years although it's unclear whether they saw much action. When James VI of Scotland became James I of England an uneasy peace followed and decreased its military importance.

Lindisfarne Castle © Gavin Duthie

It re-entered history with Charles I and the Civil War when a Captain Rugg was in command. Bizarrely, he's remembered for just two things: a huge nose, commented on by everyone who met him, and a poetic turn of phrase. He wrote a letter in rhyme to Charles complaining that the garrison had not been paid. He signed himself "The Great Commander of the Cormorants, The Geese and Ganders of these Hallowed Lands". Perhaps it was a reference to him having time to watch the local wildlife for want of military action. During the Civil War the garrison supported the Roundheads but fared no better and were still not paid.

The gun batteries remained alert during the 17th Century because of the danger from Dutch privateers, mentioned earlier in the section on Osborne's Fort. When that threat receded the Castle was left unmanned and fell into long years of dereliction.

It was in a very dilapidated state in 1901 when Edward Hudson, one of the founders of *Country Life* magazine, bought it and commissioned Sir

Edwin Lutyens to restore it as a holiday home. Using the tumbledown remains, he created the romantic, almost fairytale, building we see today. Standing under its towering walls, it's easy to imagine Rapunzel lowering her golden locks from a high window for her prince. Lutyens designed a series of rooms, some with interiors reminiscent of the styles portrayed by 17th Century Dutch masters he and Hudson so admired.

Every grand home needs a garden. Lutyens brought in his long-time collaborator, Gertrude Jeykll, to create a floral showpiece. The walled garden, formerly the garrison's vegetable patch, was created on a rise just north of the Castle. It was designed so it could be admired from the higher rooms. As Hudson and his guests were usually only present in summer, she chose plants which would flower then. National Trust gardeners, using Jeykll's original plans and sketches, have restored it to her planting design.

Jeykll was one of the delightful eccentrics of the Victorian and Edwardian eras and is said to have travelled everywhere accompanied by a pet raven. In summer today, the rocky slopes of the Castle are like a natural rock garden. It may not be as natural as it seems. Hudson regularly dropped seeds from the windows and Jeykll planted up the rock faces by packing seeds into shotgun cartridges and blasting away. This formidable lady, gun at shoulder, must have presented an intriguing sight for those lucky enough to have been present.

Hudson sold the Castle in 1921 to a London banker, Oswald Falk, and he in turn passed it on to another financier, Sir Edward de Stein, who gave it to the National Trust in 1944. Stein gave the island its first village hall, something remembered by the inclusion of its foundation stone when the new hall was built. Today the Castle is one of the most visited attractions in the north and is a regular wedding venue. Could there be anywhere more spectacular for the photographs? During 2017 repairs and weather-proofing costing £3m were carried out to ensure the future of this most iconic of Northumbrian landmarks.

Gertrude Jeykll's Garden © Nick Lewis (National Trust)

Lime
Ironstone and Coal -
a tale of doomed enterprises

Looking around the tranquil island today and breathing its crystal air, it's hard to believe it had a dirty and polluting past. The Whin Sill rocks have already been mentioned. The northern side of the island is dominated by ironstone and limestone and the farmland between by glacial clays left by the last Ice Age.

Lime had been produced by the monks from at least the 14th Century using stone from Coves Haven and coal from the Snook. It was a small-scale business to provide lime for mortar, whitewash or as a fertiliser.

By the 18th Century it had become commercial with kilns at two sites in the dunes at Chare Ends. Lime was taken by horse-drawn wagons to a jetty near St Cuthbert's Island. The remains of the kilns are still visible, the track gives access to the dunes but all trace of the jetty has vanished.

The industry expanded rapidly in the 1860s when a Dundee company built the large kilns near the Castle and the wagonway which curves northwards past the Lough to Nessend quarry. Limestone was hauled the mile or so to kilns. Ships collected coal from the Tyne and discharged it on a jetty under the Castle. This was used to burn the lime which was then shipped out to Scotland. The island population expanded rapidly and the whole area must have presented a bustling and smoky scene.

The enterprise was remarkably short-lived for such heavy investment. The last ship carrying lime departed in 1883 and the kilns were last fired in 1900 to provide lime for local farmers. The Scottish investors had become victims of the rapidly changing industrial scene with increased competition from mainland producers. They used the rapidly developing

Castle Limekilns © Robert Turner

railways to move their lime, faster, more efficiently and cheaper than ships relying on tides and weather.

The kilns, wagonway and jetty were abandoned to the elements. The kilns have been restored by the National Trust, the wagonway is now one of the island's most popular walks but all that remains of the jetty are a few skeletal wooden uprights.

Lime wasn't the only industry in the 18th and 19th Century. Ironstone was extracted around Sandham Bay and Coves Haven. But with the centre of operations covered half the time by the sea, it's no surprise that it failed. Efforts to commercially mine coal at the Snook also collapsed because seams were too thin. The tower at the Snook, now a house, covered a shaft. Another project to use local clay for brick-making reported in the Berwick Advertiser in 1864 never got off the ground.

A walk around
the East side

THE LOUGH – a fishpond for the Priory?

Lough Pond © Robert Turner

The old wagonway from the Castle lime kilns runs northwards past the Lough and towards Emmanuel Head, easternmost point of the island. The Lough is the only permanent body of fresh water and long an attraction for both people and wildlife. The monks may have created it or perhaps simply adapted an existing pool fed by springs and rainwater from the surrounding land. They may have stocked it as a year-round source of fish as a change from a diet heavily weighted towards sea fish. Eels are still attracted to the Lough and could also have provided good eating.

During the first half of the 20th Century guests at the Castle fished at the Lough. It was kept largely clear of vegetation by being regularly cleared by horse-power. Long chains were strung between horses and they were then led along its banks. The heavy chains ripped out the reeds and other cover.

Since then nature has taken over. Even in the last couple of decades the extent of open water has decreased significantly with encroachment of vigorous colonisers including Reedmace and fast-growing Phragmites. Seeds from the feathery heads of this tall grass are a winter attraction for wildfowl.

An old birdwatching hut was demolished in 2014 and the present elevated hide was built as part of the Peregrini Lindisfarne Partnership Scheme with funding from the Heritage Lottery Fund. It gives fine views across the Lough and surrounding area. It's best in the mornings when the sun is behind. The Lough is a regular breeding site for common waterside birds including Coots, Moorhens, Little Grebes and Mute Swans and occasionally Mallards, Tufted Ducks, Shovelers and Teal. It formerly held a large, raucous colony of Black-headed Gulls. The colony was deserted in 2004 when an Otter moved in, preying on eggs and chicks. Otters are wonderful to watch but are deadly for waterside birds. In 2014 around 20 pairs of gulls nested again, only to fall victim to a Fox.

Smaller species, including Reed Buntings and Sedge Warblers are regular breeders and Reed Warbles and Bearded Tits are occasionally present.

Every winter the Lough is the scene of one of nature's greatest spectacles, a huge roost of Starlings. In some years up to 40,000 fly in at dusk, often performing their spectacular shape-shifting murmurations against the sunset before pouring down like inverted smoke into the reedbeds. The roost regularly attracts predators including Barn and Short-eared owls, Kestrels, Merlins and occasionally the supreme aerial predators, Peregrines, all on the lookout for an easy meal.

Emmanuel Head

EMMANUEL HEAD - a scene of shipwrecks and tragedy

The white pyramid, visible right across the island, is a reminder of just how dangerous this stretch of coast was during the era of sailing ships and early steam-powered vessels. The 45-foot structure was built around 1810 and was one of the first day-markers around Britain's coastline. Visible from many miles at sea, it acted as a warning to mariners before the days of accurate navigation aids.

This rocky area was the scene of numerous wrecks and loss of life. Anyone seeking a salutary reminder need only examine the display boards outside the Priory Museum to see how often it featured in lifeboat callouts. An even sadder reminder is a few yards on through the churchyard gates. Immediately on the right is the grave of nine men of the crew of the steamship Holmrook who perished in 1882, shipmates in life and together in death.

The white pyramid, still given a regular coat of paint by Trinity House, is an irresistible attraction to walkers. There are memorial seats on three sides, giving fine views of a sea which has wrought so much havoc and which today remains a place of great danger. It's a wonderful spot for a short break or picnic stop on one of the quieter spots on the island. It's also possible to get shelter from all but direct easterly winds and it can certainly be very windy.

Birdwatchers often use Emmanuel Head for sea-watching. Lines of our biggest seabirds, Gannets, from the world's biggest colony on the Bass Rock in the Firth of Forth are often offshore between March and November. Many pass to and from distant fishing grounds but sometimes they pause to feed. First one and then a few birds will circle high. If shoals are visible they will start diving spectacularly headlong into the sea. Other birds will quickly be attracted and a feeding frenzy can begin, a succession of scores of white bodies hitting the surface. Gannets are superbly streamlined and close their wings just as they hit the water at speeds of up to 60mph. Nature has given them reinforced skulls to withstand the impact.

Cormorants, Shags and various terns and auks from breeding colonies on the Farne Islands are regularly attracted to join these feeding frenzies which can either be very short or can last for hours.

Immediately north of the Head is the gently curving Sandham Bay and the headland of Nessend with the quarry which revealed the island's ancient past. A short distance further on and sheltered by the island's only high cliffs is Coves Haven, terminating in Snipe Point, north-easterly point of the island.

Sandham Bay © Gavin Duthie

The North Shore

GREEN SHIEL – Anglo-Saxon farming and an extinct bird
In a wide and sloping hollow in the dunes on the edge of the North Shore are the low remains of thick walls, now partly covered by sand and vegetation. They are all that survives of what was a busy Anglo-Saxon farming settlement in the 8th Century. The area's name is interesting: "Shiel" is an old Northumbrian name for a hut or rough dwelling of the kind once used by shepherds. "Green" could just indict a stretch of fertile ground, as this area was before it was overlaid by the dunes which developed during a series of severe storms in the 15th and 16th Centuries.

The walls of thick rough blocks indicate three buildings. They were excavated in the 1980s by the Leicester University archaeologists who also discovered the pre-historic flints at Nessend quarry. Their work revealed the remains of cattle, seals and whales, deer antlers and many limpet and whelk shells. Also found was a silver penny minted in the reign of Aethelred of Wessex (866-871) and some 9th Century Northumbrian coins known as stycas. These included seven together, perhaps someone's precious savings.

Cattle-raising seemed to be the settlement's primary concern. Occupation coincided with Aidan's first monastery, leading to speculation that it might have produced the calf hides used for the Lindisfarne Gospels. Apart from a spearhead, a key, an amber bead and a fragment of a bone comb, no other personal or domestic possessions were found, perhaps indicating that the early farmers only used the site seasonally.

The seal bones and antlers indicated that hunting remained important. The whale bones may have come from stranded animals, something which occasionally occurs. In 2001 a 16-foot Minke Whale was washed up on the North Shore and a ten-foot young Beaked Whale followed at Nessend in 2006. The shellfish may have been used either for eating or fishing bait.

The bones of birds showed that they also featured in the diet. They were identified as species still common on the island today with one fascinating exception. These were the bones of a Great Auk, famously extinct since 1844 when the last was killed by Victorian collectors in Iceland. It proved that they must have been present in the North Sea. The only other local evidence comes from bones found in a cave at Whitburn 50 miles southwards and the capture of a "penguin" on the Farne Islands in 1769. From its description, experts have concluded that it was in fact a Great Auk. Green Shiel appeared to have been abandoned at about the time the monks left the island. Perhaps the farmers also decided that it would be foolish to remain in the face of constant Viking threat.

NORTH SHORE AND SNOOK – salmon fishing, grounded ships and a witch

Just beyond Green Shiel is the long and curving North Shore. It's one of the largest and finest beaches in Northumberland. It stretches unbroken for more than five miles, first along the seaward edge of the Snook and then continuing on to Goswick and Cheswick, northern boundary of the Lindisfarne National Nature Reserve. It's extremely wide at low tide when the sea is very distant.

This beautiful and unspoiled area can be reached by walking across the island or, much more easily, by using the free car park at the Snook and cutting a short distance through the dunes.

The North Shore wasn't always as tranquil as it appears today but was once the centre of a thriving salmon-fishing enterprise. Out along the ridged sandbars remain lines of wooden poles. Nets were strung between them to catch salmon moving along the coast. When the tide receded islanders would collect the trapped fish, often clambering along ropes to reach them. They were taken to the long building, now known as Snook House, for cleaning and processing.

After the Second World War one islander was offered the then redundant building but turned it down because he thought the asking price of £50 was too expensive. Now the old building and neighbouring Snook Tower have new lives as very desirable holiday homes.

The banks which held the poles proved dangerous for many ships over the centuries. But that sometimes provided a welcome source of income for the locals. In 1939 a Norwegian cargo boat Royal ran ashore in thick fog. The following year a Danish steamer, Prins Kund, met a similar fate. Both proved impossible to float off. Islanders had a solution which involved weeks of back-breaking work, often at night as dictated by tides. Working in teams, they dug deep channels and little by little the ships were edged closer to deep water. At last they were floated off and saved, the hard graft earning the islanders handsome salvage payments.

Older islanders tell a childhood tale about a witch who lived in a makeshift hut on the Snook in the 1930s. Her supposedly supernatural powers enabled her to cross from the mainland by walking on the water. She really could but she was using stilts. But seen from a distance it made a big impression on young excitable minds. She can't have been a very scary witch because some of their mothers would call to chat to her. No-one was certain where she came from or, indeed, where she went. One day she simply vanished.

The North Shore and the Snook are great places for either a long walk or just a stroll. They are also somewhere to take the children away from the obvious holiday temptations of the village.

The Causeway
Tides, danger and commonsense

The Causeway © Gavin Duthie

The only road to the village runs between the southern edge of the Snook and the saltmarsh. It crosses the South Low, one of the larger streams entering the flats, at the Causeway bridge with its white refuge box.

The opening of the Causeway in 1954 brought the island into the modern era. The Causeway and road is closed twice daily by the tides. It's safe to cross two hours before high water and then again three hours after the peak of the tide. Unfortunately, these days the Causeway is so often in the news for the wrong reasons: the tiny minority who ignore the tide tables and become stranded in their cars. It hardly needs saying, but this puts their lives and those who come to their rescue at needless risk.

The island Coastguards are called out with monotonous regularity to rescue drivers and passengers and tow their vehicles to safety. They sometimes have to call assistance from the Seahouses lifeboat and occasionally a rescue helicopter, all at huge and needless expense.

The safe crossing times are widely available. They are posted on both sides of the Causeway and there is an electronic display at the main car park at the entrance to the village and others are posted around the village. For those intending to come to the island, they are published daily in most regional newspapers and are on the internet. Annual tide-tables are available at the island Post Office.

There's really no excuse for anyone being in any doubt about when they can safely use the Causeway.

The Causeway at high tide © Gavin Duthie

The Pilgrims' Way
Traditional route to the island

This route across the sands has been used for centuries by those attracted by its rich religious connections with the northern saints. Stretching for almost three miles, it can be completed comfortably within a couple of hours. It proves one of the most fascinating walking experiences in the region, giving a real sense of peace and isolation.

The route is marked by the line of poles running from just east of the Causeway bridge to Chare Ends. Facing a twice daily battering from the tides which have been, on occasion, strong enough to shear through four-inch concrete posts on the bridge, they have to be replaced periodically. The present line and two square refuge boxes were last renewed in 1987, the 1,200th anniversary of St Cuthbert's death. The route was formerly used by islanders with ponies and traps and later old taxis to ferry visitors across, but that became redundant with the opening of the Causeway.

Sunrise over the Pilgrims' Way © Emma Rothera

Today the route is still used by pilgrims but much more commonly by walkers completing the last stage of St Cuthbert's Way from Melrose, his birthplace in the Borders. The route covers 62 miles of the finest countryside and uplands in the Borders and Northumberland. It usually takes four or five days, depending on pace and the temptation to linger and enjoy the small villages along the route. The route ends at St. Cuthbert's seat outside the St. Cuthbert's Centre. Those taking part can have a certificate stamped as proof they've completed the walk.

The route is used each Good Friday for the annual Northern Cross pilgrimage. Parties from across the north east and southern Scotland who made their way on foot to the Causeway gather for the final leg to the island. As the tide falls, they carry their wooden crosses, bare at this stage because of the solemnity of the day, across the sands. By Easter Day the crosses have been garlanded in celebration with flowers. They are carried into the parish church for the morning service. It's something which always attracts crowds.

Pilgrims' Way © *Gavin Duthie*

The traditional way to cross is bare-footed and that has advantages because even at the lowest tides there are often large areas of shallow water to cross or detour. There's a strange optical illusion to walking the Way. From the road the line of poles looks close. From the poles the road seems an awful long way off.

The route is safe, provided commonsense is used. Most importantly, work around the tide times. Safe road crossing times are widely available including at www.holyisland.northumberland.gov.uk

Here are some other tips for using the route safely:

- Ideally set off two hours before low tide, walking with the outgoing tide rather than a rising tide.

- Never attempt to cross when the tide is rising or at night or in poor weather conditions.

- Barefoot is best or wear wellingtons or walking boots that you don't mind getting very muddy.

- Tides mean that conditions underfoot vary considerably. It can be very slippery in places and a good stout stick is useful.

- Walking from Beal shore to the island it's best to cross the road bridge being mindful of traffic. At the layby on the right, looking towards the island, head out directly to the first pole on the east side of the river and follow the route to the island.

- If you don't feel confident about walking across the sands you can follow the road - although it is often extremely busy.

Wild Lindisfarne
The National Nature Reserve

The creation of the reserve in 1964 was arguably the most important decision ever made to preserve one of the region's most beautiful areas and to protect its wildlife. The area had always been important for local people and visiting sportsmen to shoot wildfowl for the pot. However, with the greater mobility of post-war years, the area was echoing to an ever-increasing number of guns and the situation was becoming unsustainable.

Local people, landowners, wildfowlers and conservations called in the then Nature Conservancy and the decision was made to create the reserve, using the ancient name of the area.

Today the reserve covering more than 8,500 acres stretching from Budle Bay northwards to Cheswick Black Rocks, includes the rich tidal zones of mud, sand and saltmarsh, island dunes and Holy Island Lough. The Lindisfarne Site of Special Scientific Interest (SSSI) extends to a further 1,800 acres, including extensive mainland dune systems. In 1976, the area was declared a Ramsar site, being of international significance and it now enjoys the highest legal levels of protection.

The reserve is managed by Natural England. It is responsible for licensing and controlling shooting and for conservation involving birds, animals and the area's incredibly rich flora. Shooting takes place between September 1st and February 20th on the northern half of Fenham Flats and Holy Island Sands. The rest of the reserve is a sanctuary. Up to 200 permits are issued annually and usually around 700 birds, mainly Wigeon and Pink-footed Geese, are shot. Islanders still operate one punt-gun and visitors occasionally bring others. These large guns are mounted on flat-bottomed boats which have to be carefully edged into position for a firing. There are old records of over 100 duck being taken with a single shot but that was a rare occurrence.

Today the reserve provides a winter home for around 50,000 Arctic wildfowl and waders, six of them in internationally important numbers, making it by far the most important wetland site in north east England.

Pale-bellied Brent Geece © Martin Kitching (northernexperienceimages.co.uk)

The reserve is the only regular British wintering ground for the Spitzbergen race of the pale-bellied Brent Goose attracting around 3,000, half the total population from this Arctic Ocean archipelago, often referred to by its Norwegian name of Svalbard. These small geese gather in large noisy flocks to graze their preferred food, Eel grass, often know by its scientific name, Zostera. The reserve is also of international importance for Pink-footed and Greylag geese, Wigeon, Bar-tailed Godwit and Grey Plover. It is nationally important for several other species.

The reserve has one breeding species of national significance, the Little Tern. One of Britain's rarest breeding seabirds, the total population is now only around 1,300 pairs. The reserve has one of only three colonies along the north east coast. Little Terns prefer to nest on open beaches, just above the high water mark. But these beaches are exactly the places visitors like to use and human pressure has evicted them from many former breeding sites.

Fortunately, the main island colony is cut off by all but the lowest tides allowing the birds to safely fledge young. The small colony is closely monitored and everything possible is done to protect the terns. In 2016 17 pairs successfully raised 38 youngsters, the best result since monitoring began in 1970.

Little Terns © Kevin Simmonds

Seals

Raging bulls and ghostly noises

The reserve is a wonderful place for watching and hearing Grey Seals. They haul out to rest and socialise in huge numbers on the Black Law, Guile Point and the sandbanks of the flats. Seen from a distance, they can appear like heaped banks of smooth black and grey rocks until, that is, they start to move. There is also the constant and rather eerie rising and falling chorus, likened variously by some to wolves or distant motorbikes while others, more kindly, regard it as singing.

The Heugh provides a grandstand to see these mass gatherings and it helps to have binoculars handy. Swimming seals are often close to the shore, usually only their black football heads showing. Others will float with head and shoulders above the surface, their way of seeing what's going on around. They are very social animals. There is constant interaction, animals flopping along to find more comfortable spots, often bickering with neighbours. Males are very much larger than female and can be very aggressive. A bull in a temper is a fearsome sight. Although most haul out in the areas south and west of the Heugh others prefer rocky areas around the north east end of the island. Small gatherings of large bulls are regular at Snipe Point jousting for the best positions.

The seals are from the breeding colony of more than 5,000 on the Farne Islands, one of the largest in Britain. Up to 2,000 pups are born between October and December. Their first fur is a delightful pale cream which quickly gives way to grey and brown. They are fed by the mothers for around three weeks on a rich diet of oily milk and quadruple in weight. During this period they are very vulnerable. They can be crushed by fighting males and storms can wash them from their rocky nurseries. At around three weeks old they are deserted by their mothers. Hunger eventually drives them into the sea to fend for themselves. It's a difficult time and around 30% perish. This rises to 50% during the first year of life. Grey seals can stay submerged for up to eight minutes and can dive to around 90 feet while hunting. Most remain fairly close to the colony but a few are wanderers. Tagged animals from the Farne Islands regularly cross the North Sea to Norway, Germany and Holland. Very small numbers of Common or Harbour Seals occur although some may be overlooked in the huge numbers of their grey cousins.

Seals may look friendly but they have very powerful jaws and sharp teeth. Most will quickly retreat into the safety or the water when disturbed. However, some will remain and should never be approached. Please enjoy them from a distance.

Grey Seal © Ian Cook

The Nature Trail
Getting close to wildlife

This three-mile trail has been organised by Natural England and starts at the Window on Wild Lindisfarne. Prominent numbered wooden posts mark suggested stopping points and it gives details of what might be found, depending on time of year. The route takes in the Castle area, the seaward end of the Crooked Lonnen, the Lough, the dune edges and the Straight Lonnen leading back to the village.

The first section provides wide views of the harbour, pier, fishing vessels and the famous upturned boats. Beyond it the Heugh and, further away, the high navigation pillars at Guile Point. Eider ducks are present throughout the year and Cormorants often sit on rocks drying their outstretched wings.

The next section uses the old lime kilns wagonway and provides extensive sea views. Waders including Oystercatchers, Redshanks and Turnstones use the rocky shore. In June and July it's worth looking out for 'crèches' of young Eider ducks. Several females will herd their young together in sheltered spots for safety.

Narrow-bordered five-spot Burnet moth © Iain Robson

Details of the Lough and its history have their own section in this guide. The hide makes a handy picnic spot or shelter if the weather is unkind. The trail's next section runs along the edge of the dunes. This area is wonderful between May and August for its range of wild flowers, particularly orchids, and for its butterflies, notably Dark-green Fritillaries, and moths, particularly the small black and red Burnet moths. More information is contained in our section on Birds, Flora and Butterflies.

The trail then turns southwards down the Straight Lonnen. The fields on the right are the regular haunt of the island population of up to 20 Roe Deer. Although mainly a woodland species, they like this open area and have raised fawns annually since 2008.

Roe Deer in the dunes © Andy Mould

Birds
A wonderful place for migration

The importance of the National Nature Reserve has already been emphasised. The island, thrusting out well into the North Sea, also attracts a host of migratory birds, some very rare. This makes it one of the north's top destinations for birdwatchers, particularly during spring and autumn migration. Holy Island has been likened in human terms to an international airport with mass arrivals and departures in every direction.

Its importance can be judged from the fact that of the 413 species of birds recorded up to 2017 in Northumberland, 35 made their first and sometimes only appearances on the island. A total of 336 species have occurred on the island and reserve, including visitors from the Arctic, Asia, North America, the Mediterranean, Middle East, South Atlantic and even the Pacific Ocean.

The island also has important populations of breeding birds, including Skylarks, Meadow Pipits and Song Thrushes, whose numbers have declined alarmingly elsewhere.

Spring migration between March and late May involves many more common species heading towards Scandinavian breeding areas but also occasionally sought-after rarities. Red-backed Shrikes, Bluethroats and rarer warblers sometimes occur at this period.

During summer, seabirds are the main attraction with Guillemots, Razorbills, Puffins and terns, mainly from the Farne Islands, regularly offshore and, of course, many Gannets already detailed in our Emmanuel Head section. Arctic and Great Skuas together with Manx and Sooty Shearwaters are usually offshore in late summer.

Barn Owl © Richard Dunn

While all these are wonderful to see, Holy Island really comes into its own in autumn. Large numbers of migrants, often thousands each day, can arrive from Scandinavia and other parts of Northern Europe and Russia. The most prominent are the northern thrushes, Fieldfares, Redwings and many northern Blackbirds. It's a wonderful experience to walk out on a red dawn in October as flock after flock pass overhead. These mass arrivals usually trigger the appearance of rarities from further east, mainly Russia and Siberia. The most regular are Yellow-browed Warblers, the island usually attracting Northumberland's highest numbers. But it's the real Siberian "gems" which can accompany them which are the greatest prize for keen birders. These include the tiny but brightly-coloured Pallas's Warblers and the more soberly plumaged Radde's Warblers, both named after early Siberian explorers. Holy Island has attracted even rarer birds from that area, including Northumberland's first Siberian Accentor. A relative of our humble Dunnock, this species had never been recorded in Britain until a small influx of around a dozen birds in autumn 2016, one of them near the North Shore. During the same period the Straight Lonnen attracted a White's Thrush, another extremely rare species from Siberia and only the third ever seen in Northumberland. The first had been on the island 102 years earlier.

During winter the island is the haunt of Short-eared Owls, patiently quartering low over the fields hunting voles. Other predators, including Peregrines and Merlins, are regularly present, often panicking waders across the flats and island fields. The sea holds the full range of sea duck, including the very attractive Long-tailed Duck and other attractive rarer species including Slavonian Grebes.

Long-tailed Duck © Tim Melling

Flora
Beautiful flowers and a unique orchid

Holy Island has a stunning flora, including an orchid found nowhere else and therefore a huge attraction for botanists. Flowers begin to appear from March, first with Wallflowers in their natural settings on village walls and rocky areas of the Heugh. Fields soon glow yellow with Lesser Celandines and there are patches of Primroses and Cowslips in the dunes.

Others soon follow with Sea Campion and Scurvy Grass and the first unfurling balls of Thrift, known locally as Sea Pinks. By June the saltmarsh along the road past the Snook is, for a short period, ablaze with pink from thousands of these hardy plants.

During summer, village walls are bright with Red Valerian and Stonecrops while their sunny faces are patched with the pale blue of Ivy-leaved Toadflax. Plants associated with Whin Sill grasslands include Rockrose and Haresfoot Clover. Meadow Saxifrage was first recorded on the Heugh in 1807 and still flourishes, an example of the tenacity of plants.

However, the dunes, particularly areas damp from winter flooding, hold the real floral treasures of the island, particularly orchids. The island has ten species, a range unrivalled in the region. They include Early Purple, Common Spotted, Early Marsh, Northern Marsh, Pyramidal, Common Twayblade, Marsh Helleborine and the unique Lindisfarne Helleborine. There are a few Coralroot Orchids at the Snook and a tiny patch of Frog Orchids near Nessend quarry.

Pyramidal Orchid © David Feige

The Lindisfarne Helleborine has been given the scientific name *Epipactis sancta,* an appropriately religious title for something unique to the cradle of Christianity in the north. Previously it was regarded as a Dune Helleborine with the island only one of a handful of sites in Britain. In 2003, during research into Britain's orchids, DNA sampling was carried out. To the amazement of those involved, it was discovered that the island plants differed genetically and organically from Dune Helleborines elsewhere and deserved their special status.

The Snook also has an impressive patch of Round-leaved Wintergreen. Across the island, the dunes hold Carline Thistles, Autumn Gentians tall and stately blue and purple Vipers Bugloss and in late summer the tiny cupped pink flowers of Seaside Centuary. The appearance along the dune paths of the silvery white flowers of Grass of Parnassus is a sign that autumn is approaching.

Holy Island has a highly invasive problem plant, Pirri-pirri Bur, a native of New Zealand. The most likely explanation for its presence is that seeds arrived on wool imported to mills along the Tweed. Washed out during processing and carried out to sea by the river, seeds washed ashore and rapidly colonised the Snook and then spread to the rest of the island.

The spiny seeds cling to clothing, animal fur and birds' feathers with a tenacity that has to be experienced to be believed. Warning signs, aimed particularly at dog walkers, are prominently displayed. Methods are being sought to get rid of this troublesome newcomer which can overwhelm the native flora.

Pirri-pirri Bur © Raine Bryant

Marsh Helleborine © Martin Kitching (northernexperienceimages.co.uk)

Butterflies and Moths
Beauty on the wing

The presence of so many nectar-rich flowers attracts a profusion of butterflies and moths. At a time of concern about dwindling numbers of some of our most beautiful and once plentiful butterflies, the island supports good populations of Ringlets, Meadow Browns, Wall Browns, Small Tortoiseshells, Large, Small and Green-veined whites, Common Blues and Small Coppers. Recently, species associated with gardens, including Peacocks, Red Admirals and Commas have increased. Speckled Woods are comparative newcomers as part of their northward expansion. Painted Ladies can be abundant during their periodic invasions from North Africa.

The most spectacular of the island's butterflies are the orange and black Dark Green Fritillaries. The island has Northumberland's highest population and they are one of the joys of walking through the dunes on

Dark Green Fritillary © Tim Melling

warm days in June and July. Concentrations of over 200 have been found in a survey patch of just 50 square metres north of the Straight Lonnen where they are attracted by abundant path-side patches of Red and White clovers. They are a really wonderful creature to watch.

Small numbers of cunningly camouflaged Graylings are also present, usually in the more bare and sandy areas of the dunes. They have a wonderful ability to settle, tilt sideways and vanish, an adaption to avoid predators.

Two species of day-flying moths are abundant. The red and black Six-spot Burnets are often present in their thousands. Cinnabar moths are also common, often indicated by the presence of balls of writhing yellow and black caterpillars on the flower heads of Ragwort. Hummingbird Hawkmoths are occasionally attracted to village gardens.

The island also has the full range of night-flying moths, including Elephant and Small Elephant hawk moths, Poplar Hawkmoth, Garden Tigers, Ghost Moth, Swallowtail, White and Buff Ermines and many smaller species including Silver Y, Burnished Brass and Gold Spot.

Cinnabar Moth caterpillar on Ragwort © Stewart Sexton

Rock Pools
A miniature wonderland

The southern and eastern sides of the island are rocky. Hundreds of rock pools left by the receding tide provide happy hunting grounds for the young and not so young. Rock-pooling is always fascinating. Turn over a stone and you never know what might pop out. The pools provide myriads of sea anemones, translucent shrimps, tiny fish and small crabs all left temporarily stranded. They also hold an abundance of limpets and other shellfish. A granddaughter of the writer calls the pools alongside the pier "Shells Galore" for that very reason.

A Rock Pool

The tideline of the island's beaches, near St Cuthbert's Island, Sandham Bay, Coves Haven and particularly the North Shore, are also wonderful places to search for various shells and the occasional sea urchins and cuttlefish bones.

Cuttlefish Bone © Iain Robson

More scientifically, the spectacular coastline of Berwickshire and North Northumberland is very important, not just for the local fishing industry but also for marine conservation. During bad weather the North Sea can appear to be a dangerous, grey and forbidding place and in reality a dangerous one too. But this conceals a dazzling array of colourful marine life and plants. The shallow seas along this stretch are the location of a huge rocky reef which for those who dive forms an almost magical seascape teeming with life.

Due to the importance of these waters, this stretch which includes Holy Island, is now protected as a European Marine Site. Further north, the area around Eyemouth and St Abbs Head, which are very popular with divers because of the clarity of the water, have been designated a Voluntary Marine Reserve.

Dark Skies
A myriad of stars
and the Northern Lights

Holy Island is one of the darkest places along the Northumberland coast, making it ideal for star gazing. For anyone from towns and cities with high levels of light pollution, to walk out on a clear night is really exhilarating. The whole sky can be bejewelled and it's one of the prime sites for one of nature's most fabulous spectacles, the Aurora Borealis or Northern Lights.

Then, usually for a brief period, the north eastern horizon can pulsate with pink, blue and green, an unforgettable experience.

These days it's easier than ever with scientific institutions providing free Aurora alerts via the internet and mobile phones, grading them from possible to probable and giving likely geographical locations.

With the sea stretching the whole east side of the coast, it means that even in local towns and villages it's possible to appreciate the darkness of local skies. The Causeway is always popular although care must be taken with the tides.

The island itself is even better. It's only necessary to walk out of the village towards the Castle to appreciate the kind of darkness which has been lost to so much of Britain. Apart from the low, regular sweep of the Longstone lighthouse, there is no light pollution to mar the sky and it really shows.

The AONB Partnership actively promotes star-watching events in co-operation with the Northumberland Astronomical Society (NASTRO). Details appear on its website and in the local press. Early booking is wise and these events fill up fast.

Milky Way over Holy Island © Dru Dodd

Nearby Attractions
History, art and wildlife

Holy Island is a convenient base from which to visit some of the area's other attractions, including busy small towns, fishing villages and historic sites. For walkers and visitors in general, the official guide book for the Northumberland Coast Path is invaluable.

The area's largest towns and shopping centres are Berwick-upon-Tweed and Alnwick. Because of its commanding position on the Border, Berwick has a turbulent history and repeatedly changed hands during conflicts between England and Scotland. Its Elizabethan walls are intact and walking around them gives panoramic views of the old town, the river famed for its salmon fishing and the open sea.

The artist, L. S. Lowry, famous for his "matchstick men" depictions of industrial Manchester, regularly holidayed in Berwick from the mid-1930s until shortly before his death in 1976. He produced over 20 local paintings and drawings. There's a Lowry Trail with display boards taking visitors around his locations so they can see them through the artist's eyes.

Walking the Lowry Trail at Berwick-upon-Tweed © Gavin Duthie

The historic town of Alnwick has its famous Castle, seat of the Dukes of Northumberland, and, just as well-known these days, the Alnwick Gardens. The town's old railway station houses Barter Books, one of Britain's biggest second-hand bookshops.

Southwards from Holy Island is Bamburgh, one-time capital of Northumbria. Now a busy village, it's completely dominated by its huge towering castle. Grace Darling, heroine of the Farne Islands, is buried in the local churchyard and a small museum opposite tells her dramatic story.

Three miles further on is the busy fishing port of Seahouses, departure point for the Farne Islands, internationally important for their seabird colonies which include everyone's favourites, Puffins, with over 20,000 breeding pairs. A trip during the breeding season between April and July is a wonderful experience. Inner Farne, scene of St Cuthbert's death has a small beautiful chapel as well as very aggressive breeding Arctic Terns. Remember to take your hat. They are very bold defenders of their eggs and young.

Winter walk at Bamburgh © Gavin Duthie

Further Reading
History, religion and archaeology

Lindisfarne: the Cradle Island by Magnus Magnusson, Oriel Press 1984

St Cuthbert, His Cult and His Community to AD 1200 by Gerald Bonner
David Rollson and Clare Stancliffe, Boydell Press 1989

Lindisfarne Holy Island by Deirdre O'Sullivan and Robert Young
English Heritage 1995

The Tides of Time: Archaeology on the Northumberland Coast by Caroline Hardie
and Sara Rushton, Northumberland County Council, 2000 and 2004

*Exploring the Geology and Landscapes of the Northumberland Coast Area
of Outstanding Natural Beauty,* AONB Partnership 2005

*Exploring the Historic Buildings of the Northumberland Coast Area of Outstanding
Natural Beauty,* AONB Partnership 2006

The Story of Holy Island by Kate Tristram, Canterbury Press 2009

Wildlife
A Naturalist on Lindisfarne by Richard Perry, Lindsay Drummond, 1964

Birdwatching on the Northumberland Coast by Tom Cadwallender
AONB Partnership 2003 and 2016

The Birds of Holy Island & Lindisfarne National Nature Reserve by Ian Kerr
NatureGuides, 2016 and 2017

Walking
The Northumberland Coast Path Official Guide by Iain Robson
AONB Partnership 2005, 2009 and 2013

Notes